Lady Kimberly Motes Doty

What is God's Greatest Commandment?

Through the captivating adventures of Aurora, Honor, and Cade, young readers will discover the profound significance of these commandments and how they can make a difference in their own lives and in the world around them.

ISBN 979-8-8690-6033-4 (paperback)
ISBN 979-8-8690-6034-1 (digital)

Lady Kimberly Industries LLC
15019 Madeira Way, #86174
Madeira Beach, Florida 33708-9998

https://ladykimberlyindustries.godaddysites.com/

Once upon a time, in a beautiful village, there lived three cousins, named Aurora, Conor, and Cade.

They loved playing together and exploring the world around them.

One sunny day, as they were playing near a big oak tree, they noticed a book lying on the ground.

Curious, they picked it up and saw that it was a special book called the Bible.

As they opened the book, they discovered something amazing – commandments!

They learned that commandments were like rules that God gives us to help us live in a purposeful and fulfilling way.

Living a purposeful and fulfilling life means finding meaning and happiness in everything we do.

It means doing things that make us happy, helping others, and making a positive impact on the world around us. It's about discovering our passions and talents, and using them to make a difference.

When we live a purposeful and fulfilling life, we feel satisfied, content, and proud of ourselves.

It's like finding our own special way to make the world a better place.

The Bible had so many commandments, over six hundred bible verses full of them!

Wow, that was a lot of commandments!

But the children also learned that there were two commandments that were the most important.

The first one was to love God with all their heart, soul, and mind.

This meant that they should love God with everything they had, like their feelings, thoughts, and their whole being.

They realized that loving God meant talking to Him, thanking Him for the beautiful world, and being kind to others.

The second important commandment was to love their neighbors as themselves.

This meant treating other people with kindness and love, just like they would want to be treated.

They understood that being a good neighbor meant helping others, sharing, and being friendly.

Excited to learn more, the children read a story in the Bible about Jesus.

Jesus was asked which commandment was the most important, and He gave a very special answer.

He said that loving God with all their heart, soul, and mind was the first and great commandment.

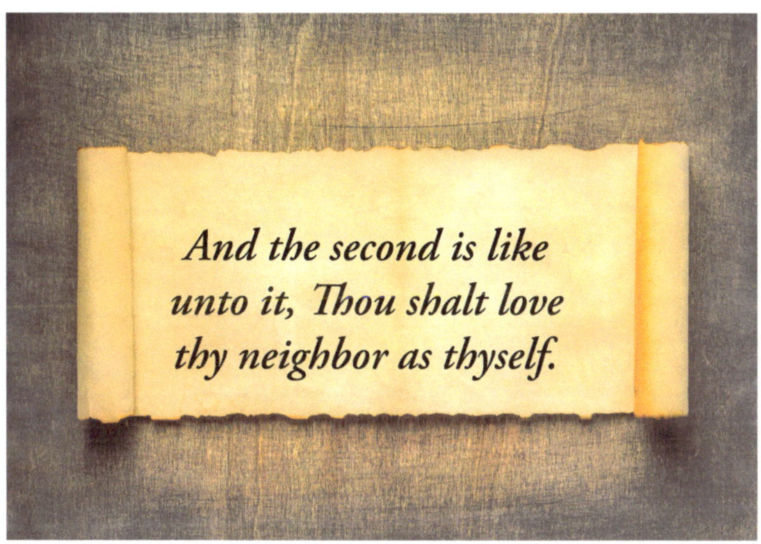

But He didn't stop there!

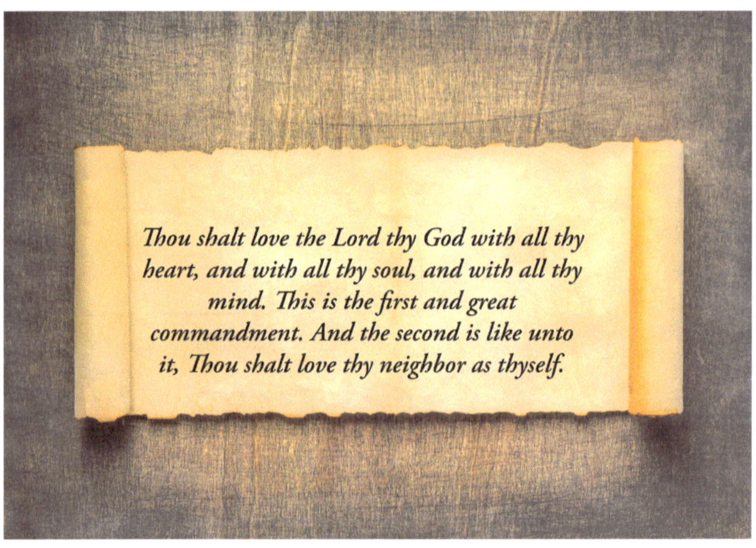

He also said that loving their neighbors as themselves was just as important!

Aurora, Conor, and Cade were inspired by Jesus' words.

They realized that the most important
thing they could do was to love God
and love others.

They decided to put these commandments into
action in their everyday lives.

They started by saying a prayer every day, thanking God
for His love and asking for guidance.

They also showed kindness to their neighbors, helping them with their chores, sharing their toys, and being good friends.

As they followed these commandments, something magical happened.

The village became a happier and more loving place.

Everyone noticed the kindness and love that Aurora, Conor, and Cade showed.

Then they started following the commandments too.

The children realized that by loving God and loving others, they were making a positive difference in the world.

They understood that these commandments were not just rules to follow, but a way to live a meaningful and fulfilling life.

From that day forward, Aurora, Conor and Cade
continued to love God with all their heart,
soul, and mind, and they always treated
          others with kindness and love.

They became shining examples
of how following the commandments could
bring joy and harmony to their village.

And so, the children lived happily ever after, spreading love and kindness wherever they went, guided by the two most important commandments from the Bible.

Love God with all your heart, soul and mind.

Love thy neighbor as thyself.

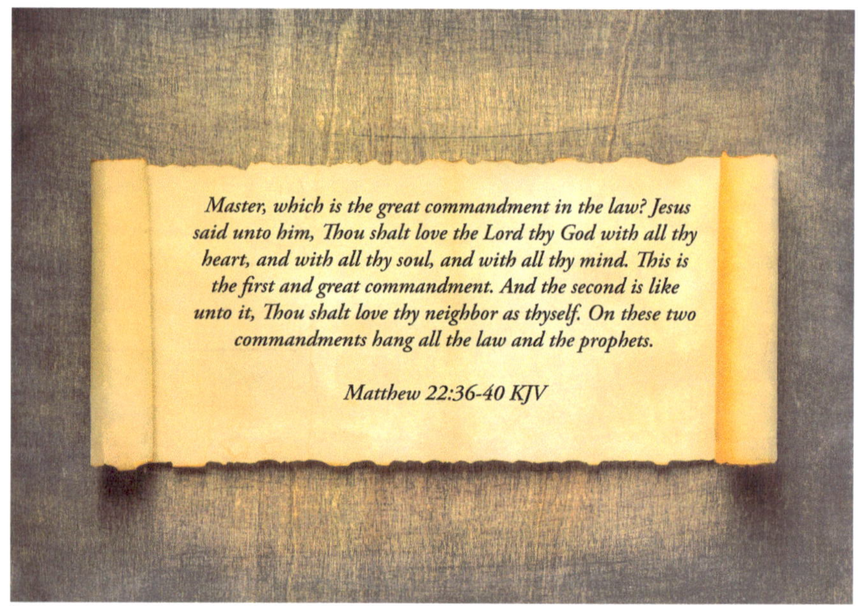

Master, which is the great commandment in the law? Jesus
said unto him, Thou shalt love the Lord thy God with all thy
heart, and with all thy soul, and with all thy mind. This is
the first and great commandment. And the second is like
unto it, Thou shalt love thy neighbor as thyself. On these two
commandments hang all the law and the prophets.

Matthew 22:36-40 KJV

About the Author

Lady Kimberly Motes Doty has dedicated her life to helping people in many different ways.

She is a minister, which means she helps others find their spiritual path.

She is also a life coach, which means she guides people to live their best lives.

Lady Kimberly is even a natural health specialist, which means she knows a lot about taking care of our bodies and staying healthy.

In addition to all of this, she loves to write and share her wisdom with others.

When she's not working, she enjoys spending time with her family.

https://ladykimberlyindustries.godaddysites.com/

https://mybook.to/LadyKimberlyBooks

More Lady Kimberly Children's Books

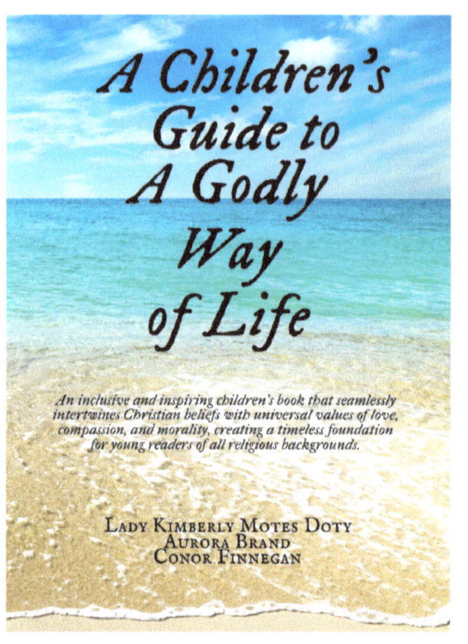

Introducing children to the wonders of God and the teachings of the Bible is a vital aspect of their spiritual development. That's why "A Children's Guide to A Godly Way of Life" is the ideal resource to nurture their curiosity and guide them towards a deeper understanding of faith. By introducing them to the commandments and the valuable lessons Jesus taught us about living a godly life, we can provide them with a solid foundation in their spiritual journey.

"A Children's Guide to a Godly Way of Life" is not just another ordinary book. It is a treasure trove of knowledge and wonder, carefully crafted to quench the thirst for understanding that resides within every child's soul. With each turn of the page, their imagination will ignite, propelling them on a lifelong voyage of love and devotion to God, and an insatiable hunger for unraveling the mysteries of the divine.

"Discovering God's Love: A Magical Journey of Faith and Wonder"

Introducing a captivating new children's book series by the talented author, Lady Kimberly Motes Doty. "Discovering God's Love" is an exploration of God's love and teachings through enchanting and relatable stories that conveys the sense of curiosity and discovery that young readers will experience as they delve into each book. "Discovering God's Love" emphasizes the spiritual growth and lifelong connection with God. The first five books in the series have been released with the full series to include short stories about the commandments, how to treat others, how to treat animals, and our own personal growth with God.

This extraordinary collection aims to teach children about God's boundless love and His teachings from the Bible through enchanting short stories. Lady Doty has masterfully crafted these tales to speak directly to children in a language they can easily understand, making each book both Biblically based and effortlessly relatable.

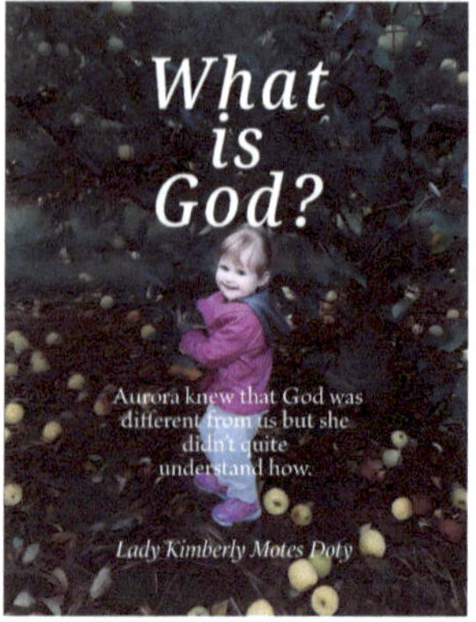

"What is God?" is a captivating children's book that follows the curious and kind-hearted girl, Aurora, on a quest to uncover the answer to a timeless question: What or who is God?

"Where is God?" is a heartwarming children's book that follows the journey of Aurora, a curious young girl, as she seeks to understand the presence of God. Wondering where God is, Aurora embarks on a quest to discover His whereabouts.

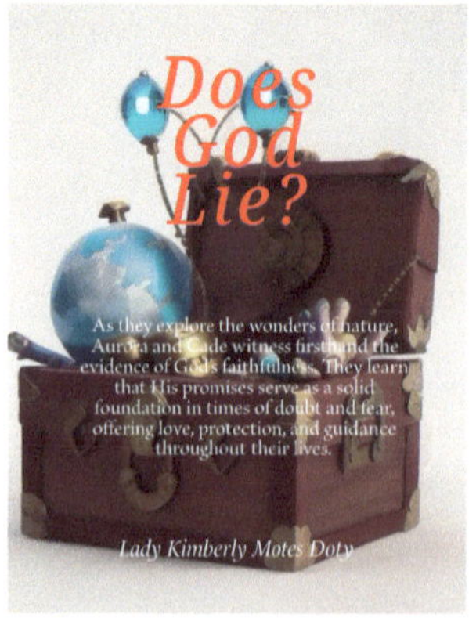

"Does God Lie?" is a heartwarming tale that follows the journey of two siblings, Aurora and Cade, as they stumble upon a mysterious old book about God's promises. Intrigued by the idea of unwavering faithfulness, they embark on a quest to learn more about the reliability of God's word.

Join Aurora, Cade, and Conor on a thrilling treasure hunt that takes them on a journey through the wonders of God's creation in "Is Everything God Does Good?" This heartwarming story reminds young readers of the beauty and love found in God's creations and the importance of being good stewards of the natural world.

"What Are Angels?" is a heartwarming children's book that explores the concept of angels and their role in our lives. Through the eyes of a curious little boy named Cade, author Lady Kimberly Motes Doty takes young readers on a journey of discovery and understanding.

Cade's fascination with angels leads him to ask his mother about their purpose and how they keep us safe. In response, his loving mother imparts wisdom and shares stories from the Bible. She explains that angels, although invisible to the human eye, are like invisible superheroes sent by God to watch over and protect us.

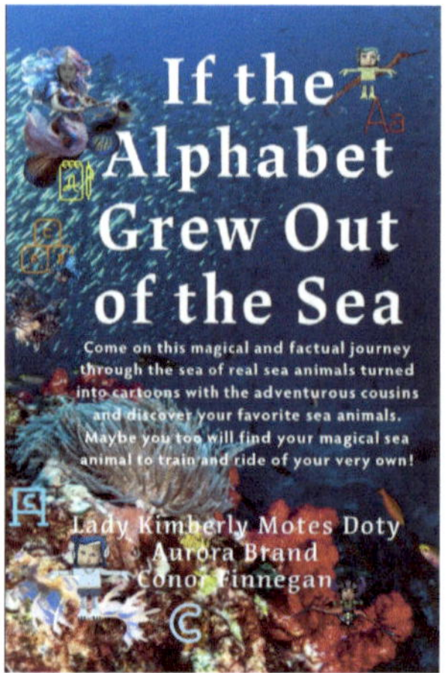

"If The Alphabet Grew Out of The Sea v2" - Almost 600 pages of mazes, word searches and fun facts about sea animals on an exciting Sea Adventure!

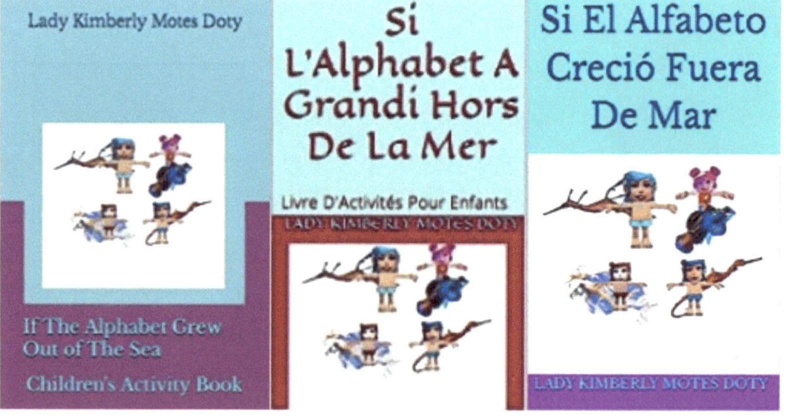

"If the Alphabet Grew Out of The Sea" V1 - in English, French & Spanish

9 798869 060334